See what I mean

Seventy-six stories, sketches and visuals for all-age services

Jonathan Mortimer

CONTENTS

How to use this workbook	4
Before you say a word	6
Part one: Show me how	**7**
Signs of life	8
Close encounters	14
Story-times	20
Part two: Tell us a story!	**25**
Some stories to tell	26
Response stories	30
Simple dramas	32
Dramas to work at	37
Dramas for all seasons	43
Index of subjects	47

Copyright © 1998 CPAS

First edition 1998

All rights reserved. The material in this book is copyright and may not be photocopied without permission from CPAS. However, permission is given for the owner of this book to copy pages for use by groups in which he or she is participating.

Published by CPAS
Athena Drive
Tachbrook Park
WARWICK
CV34 6NG

Edited and designed by AD Publishing Services
Printed by Unigraph Printing Services
Cover designed by Wild Associates

ISBN 1 8976 6085 5
British Library Cataloguing-in-Publication Data
A catalogue record for this book is available from the British Library

Church Pastoral Aid Society
Registered Charity No 1007820
A company limited by guarantee

INTRODUCTION

There comes a dreaded moment in some church services when the leader says: 'This is for the children.' Everyone braces themselves for another feverish outbreak of 'creativity', especially the children: drama that has you squirming inside, visual aids that don't aid anyone, action songs that patronize everyone (if I really were a butterfly, I'd thank the Lord I didn't have to sing that song again), and quiz questions to which the answer is always Jesus.

And yet, like treasure hidden in a muddy field, there are moments when something 'for the children' has grabbed our imagination and touched our hearts. We still remember it. It was as though we were being shown something we had never seen before. Maybe it was a child's prayer, a picture, or a story; it touched a chord somewhere deep within and played a rather beautiful note.

The God who made our imaginations can speak to them. There is a child in each of us who longs to be shown rather than spoken to, intrigued rather than taught, enchanted rather than indoctrinated. So, let's get visual!

Jesus did. He was always showing people what he meant. He pointed out to his disciples a widow and her mite, he stood a child in their midst, and he showed his enemies a Roman coin. He told his disciples to remember him with bread and wine. Knowing that actions speak louder than words, he walked on water, he calmed a storm, he fed huge crowds. Instead of saying 'God is love', he showed it. Then he might have said, 'See what I mean?'.

Even with his words, he was painting pictures. A few deft strokes from his verbal palette conjured up scenes and characters and story-lines which remain fresh twenty centuries later. A longing father, a field of rocks and thistles, bridesmaids waiting for the wedding party – someone has said that if Jesus wasn't God, surely his script-writer must have been. His pictures were worth a thousand words!

Pictures and stories and all things bright and visual are not just 'for the children'. We know they love the visual, the dramatic, the story, the non-abstract. But we all respond to them. The fact that over twelve million people regularly watch *Eastenders* and *Coronation Street* suggests there might be an audience for a good story-line. Heads jerk out of a bored slumber the moment a speaker addresses something other than our intellect. The chances are that what you remember about the services you have been to over the last month will be thoughts that were communicated with a picture of some kind.

Of course, there is a risk that with anything dramatic, entertaining, visual and different the medium can become the message, and we find ourselves praying: 'O Lord, give me a verse to go with this great visual aid.' It's then we know we're on the wrong track. But the God who created the universe has created us to communicate his Son, his good news, and it takes more than just words to do that.

HOW TO USE THIS WORKBOOK

This is a book of windows. The purpose of windows is to see through them. If they don't give you a better view, you need new ones. The ideas in this book are meant to give you and your congregation a good view (perhaps even one you had not seen before) of an old message and a living God. If they entertain, surprise, grab the attention, require participation, get you thinking, arouse curiosity, they have fulfilled their aim.

Someone might say: 'But they're not exactly getting to grips with the text or teaching us something, are they?' That would be like me test-driving a Ferrari and telling the salesman: 'The acceleration's not bad, but it doesn't have much boot-space, does it?' 'No sir,' says the salesman, 'Ferraris aren't designed for that.'

In the same way, illustrations are meant to be teasers, allusions; they don't cross all the T's and dot all the I's, but they do help you look in a certain direction. They are windows designed to frame the view but not necessarily to say much about it. But as a result the spectator should want to explore it more closely, perhaps by getting a telescope, going outside and walking around the area, or checking the view through different windows from different angles.

Part One of this book contains ideas suitable for any church service or event where you can 'get visual'. Only you know when that will be possible. A Family Service is one obvious occasion; youth services, assemblies, 'seeker' events for people from outside the church, concerts, harvest suppers – in fact on any occasion when public speaking is involved, a wisely-chosen visual illustration can only enhance the message. Windows aren't just for computers – your talks and sermons could do with them as well.

There are ten different Gospel passages arranged under three themes ('Signs of life', 'Close Encounters' and 'Story-times'). For each passage a number of ideas are given to put across the point of the passage. Obviously you cannot use them all in one service, but several of them could make a big impact and reinforce the message considerably.

The items are grouped under the following headings and symbols:

⬇ STARTER
This is usually some sort of static visual symbol which is on show throughout the event, and can be referred to on more than one occasion. To arrange the church 'geography' in a certain way before people arrive can alert everyone to the message that the service or event is aiming to communicate. A simple acetate on the overhead projector, a loaf of bread visible at the front of church, a road-sign hanging up: they can get people thinking and preparing for what is to come.

👓 VISUAL
Instead of describing something, show it! A library book, a relay baton, a champagne bottle, a picture of a spider: when someone over Sunday lunch is trying to remember what you said, it will help if they have a picture in their mind's eye of what you were getting at. A video clip can be a brilliant illustration, and with young people especially it can be very effective. But if all you are doing is holding attention, you leave your listeners saying: 'Nice video, I wonder why we watched it?'

👍 ACTION
Children do not like sitting still. So allow them to move if it helps to put across the point of what you're saying. Some of the suggestions are games, some require (optional) participation from everyone present, some just need volunteers to come up to the front. Activity games may not work in every church, so each idea suggested in this book could be altered to become just a visual aid. Then you play the game on your own, or with some primed volunteers. This reduces the risk of chaos, but also reduces the fun and possible impact.

✸ ATTENTION GRABBER
Some tricks are magic, but the teaching point

that follows must be made very well – otherwise the trick is all that gets remembered. Most tricks must be practised. Tommy Cooper might have got away with messing them up, but nobody else can.

MIME

Mimes can be very simple. For these, you can ask for volunteers on the spur of the moment. But if the mime is at all complicated, prime the volunteers you need beforehand. Mime can be especially good for Lower (Primary) School assemblies. Treat your mime artists like all your volunteers: they are gold-dust, and if you ever patronize or make fun of them, you don't deserve any help ever again.

? QUIZ

The quizzes ask a number of simple questions before making a point about them. The point of the quiz is not so much to get right answers, as to start people thinking in a certain direction.

☺ DRAMA

This is a cross-reference to one of the dramas included in Part Two.

In **Part Two** are some dramas which link with the themes in Part One. Most are simple – they can be done with a minimum of props, expertise and rehearsals. Others (marked ★★) need lines to be learnt and some rehearsing to get them right. There are also some original stories which could be used. In some ways these are more risky than drama, because you need a good story-teller to do them well.

In **both sections**, most 'windows' include a note about:

PREPARATION LEVEL

This shows how much work they require. Most are marked ★ which means they take practically no time to prepare. ★★ means they need some planning. ★★★ is for those who have technological resources (such as video projectors) and acting expertise.

POINT

This describes the view the 'window' is meant to be showing. If you want people to see another view, use another window.

Each window usually begins with some tips (in italics) of what sort of audience would appreciate this type of window, and also what dangers there are in using it. Some are like stained-glass windows which need background knowledge to appreciate; some are like those that are too high up for children to see through; others are so low that teenagers and adults will feel they're beneath them. Some are like port-holes, and give very limited vision.

At the end of the book, ideas are listed by subject (which is why each window has a number). A truth about 'Sin', for example, could be illustrated by several different windows; this index will tell you where to find them.

BEFORE YOU SAY A WORD...

A story has power to teach, inspire, and change attitudes. Everyone listens to good stories. They sell magazines, fill cinemas and line the shelves of video shops and booksellers. Small wonder they were the major teaching vehicle of Jesus. His parables opened up hearts and minds to possibilities about God.

But before you import stories and sketches into your church, ask the following questions about your prospective 'performance'.

1 Can it be seen and heard?

If the answer is 'no', you're wasting everyone's time. Your performers need audible voices, and their actions need to be deliberate and visible. Investment in radio microphones and staging blocks is a good idea.

2 What is the point of this sketch or story?

If the item is any of the following, don't contemplate it:
- nothing to do with the rest of the service
- entertainment to keep people awake (unless it's part of an entertainment event)
- the result of campaigning from the drama group to do their favourite sketch.

If it makes people think any of the following, it's likely to be serving a purpose:
- 'I've been in that situation.'
- 'I wonder what the meaning of that is?' (The talk or teaching slot will tell them.)
- 'I wonder what will happen next?'

3 Would I be happy if a visitor I brought to church saw this?

Some people have a gift for drama and storytelling, and some don't. Be sure you have enough people with enough talent for your chosen item. A sketch requires someone directing it who knows what is naff.

You can't describe 'naffness'. But its effect is that everyone longs for the item to end; nobody keeps eye-contact with the performers; nobody remembers anything of it.

Sketches are naff when, for example, the acting is wooden, when actors haven't learnt their lines or when they've learnt them parrot-fashion, or when they're not comfortable with being on stage. Even if the acting is brilliant, sketches are also naff when they start to get unbelievable. It happens when Christian drama tries to explain itself and turns 'preachy'. Remember the purpose is to provoke questions, not answer them.

The art of the story-teller is even trickier. Again, it takes someone to know what is not going to work and to kindly tell the performer(s) before they make fools of themselves. However, when teenagers or children are the performers, their involvement tells a story in itself. If you're happy with the content of the sketch, if they've worked hard at it and are now ready to take part, let them. If the plug has to be pulled, it must be done early at rehearsal stage.

4 Am I fully aware of the consequences of using drama and story?

Be aware of your congregation or audience. There is a narrow dividing line between what is dramatic (and surprises people) and what alienates. What worked at Spring Harvest might not go down well at St Cedric's. You are asking performers to invest their free time and risk their reputations. It's a high cost. Make sure their performance ties in with the rest of the service or event so that the cost is worthwhile.

PART ONE

SHOW ME HOW!
ILLUSTRATING STORIES FROM THE GOSPELS

This section gives ideas for services based on three themes from the Gospels. The first, Signs of life, looks at ways of illustrating three of Jesus' miracles that John records in his Gospel. The second is called Close encounters, and covers significant meetings Jesus had with different people which changed the course of their lives. The third, Story-times, is based on three parables which Jesus told.

SIGNS OF LIFE

THE WEDDING AT CANA

 Reading: John 2:1-11
Title: 'Don't bring a bottle'
'It's a miracle!'
'Who drank all the wine?'

1 STARTER
Road signs

Used best in a service-setting where at least some of your congregation are familiar with the signs. You may wish to have them always visible, as a constant reminder of the point you want to make.

Put a red road-sign at the front of church with the word STOP on it. Have another sign with a PETROL PUMP LOGO and a third sign saying SERVICES.

POINT There are times on our journey through life when we stop. Sometimes we are forced into doing so (show STOP sign), for example when we are ill. Sometimes we know we're getting near the end of our resources and need 'topping up' (show PETROL PUMP logo) and refreshment (show SERVICES sign).

Often, when we come to the end of our resources we discover the beginning of God's. That was what happened at Cana when the wine ran out, and Jesus' mother pointed the helpless wine-waiters to the person she knew could help.

PREPARATION LEVEL ★★ Prepare signs in advance, large enough for people at the back of church to see.

2 MIME
Exercisers

A simple, funny, visual and effective means for getting the point across for all ages. Teenager-friendly.

Four actors stand on stage, with their backs to the audience. One after the other they turn round and begin their own 'discipline'. One runs on the spot; Two lies down and lifts weights; Three starts to juggle with three balls; Four holds their breath.

Soon One gets tired and has to stop; Two can't lift the weights any longer; Three drops the balls; Four must take a breath.

POINT This makes the same point as 1 above. The waiters and hosts at the wedding of Cana had reached their wits' end. They were desperate, facing a potential social catastrophe. Jesus' sign was a catering triumph and also revealed who he was. It takes a disaster or a failure for many people to turn to God for help, and maybe experience him for the first time.

PREPARATION LEVEL ★★ Get volunteers beforehand, and rehearse them. They should include someone who can juggle a little, and someone who knows something about weights.

3 ATTENTION GRABBER
Turn the tumblers

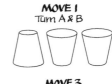

8

Put three tumblers in a line on a table. The middle one faces down, the two outside face up. You tell the congregation that the aim of the trick is to make all three tumblers face down after three moves. You are allowed to turn two tumblers with each move as the diagram shows.

Ask a volunteer to come and do the same, but make sure that the tumbler in the middle is facing up, the outer two down. This makes the trick impossible.

POINT Some magic tricks you might be able to work out, but others are not so easy. If you know the trick, this one is impossible to fail at; if you don't know it, it's impossible to succeed. The situation at the wedding was impossible; the people there had run out of options. What was needed was not a magician's trick but a miracle, a totally new way of dealing with the problem. Jesus performed this miracle not to show he was a magician, but God's Son (verse 11).

PREPARATION LEVEL ★ Get three glass tumblers on a table and practise a fast, witty performer's delivery.

4 ACTION
Winetasters

If you use wine, check with the person who gets it that they don't mind. You need fairly articulate people to get this to work. With younger audiences use the alternative below.

Bring to the front three volunteers who have been primed beforehand. Blindfold them and give them a glass of something to taste. The first two get water, the third gets wine or squash. Each must try to describe what they drink.

POINT Water is... boring, tasteless, drab (or whatever words your volunteers use). Yes, it's basically pretty watery. Wine (or squash) is... fruity, mellifluous, smooth (or whatever words were used). They are both hard to describe, but there is a great difference between them – like the difference between a shopping-list and a Shakespeare play. Through this first sign Jesus shows what a difference he has come to make.

PREPARATION LEVEL ★ Prepare the glasses and contents. Get the volunteers, possibly just before the service, but tell them what is going to happen, to make sure they are happy with it.

5 ACTION
The real thing

For a child-friendly, teenager-friendly variant on no. 4, use volunteers who reckon they are cola experts. Blindfolded as above, they each get to taste three different types of cola – a cheap brand, one that has been opened and lost its fizz, and 'the real thing'. They have to guess which is the best.

POINT Jesus didn't just make ordinary wine out of the water. That would have been amazing enough, especially as it was usual to serve cheaper wine at the end of a wedding. He produced the best, a classic vintage. It takes a cola expert to recognize 'the real thing'. The wedding guests at Cana all knew that the wine and the one who had produced it were special.

PREPARATION LEVEL ★★ Buy three different types of cola.

6 VISUAL
Thirst quencher

Best used with people who appreciate champagne. The 'champagne moment' idea is taken from the Test Match Special team on Radio Four who choose the most perfect moment of the Test Match, and award whichever cricketer performed it a bottle of bubbly.

The service leader says they need a drink and asks if anyone has some water they could sip from. Someone from the congregation brings out a bottle of champagne in an ice-bucket and champagne glass on a cloth-covered tray.

POINT All you really needed was a glass of water, the champagne really wasn't necessary. But it was a very beautiful thought. At Cana the hosts didn't really need the best wine, and probably not 180 gallons of it either. There are 'champagne moments' in life when God overwhelms us by his overflowing love and limitless generosity.

PREPARATION LEVEL ★★ More expensive than time-consuming; buy a bottle of champagne and organize the ice bucket, tray, and someone to bring it to the front on cue.

THE FEEDING OF THE 5,000

Reading: John 6:1-15
Title: '5,000 ways to use a packed lunch'
'Second helpings plus'
'Fast food for 5,000'
'Has anyone seen my sandwiches?'

7 STARTER
Use your loaf

Put a loaf of bread on a table at the front of the church as a visual reminder of what the service will be about.

PREPARATION LEVEL ★

8 ACTION
Share it round

You could get everyone talking during this. It's good for breaking up a service with movement and talk.

Ask for volunteers to cut up the loaf, and then to hand out pieces of the bread so everyone will get some.

POINT It would take a miracle to feed the church with this! How much did you get? Imagine how the disciples felt when they looked at the hungry crowds, then looked at the little packed lunch, then looked at Jesus.

PREPARATION LEVEL ★ Have bread, knife (knives) and plates or baskets ready. Ask for volunteers on the spot.

9 ACTION
Thumb marks

This is good for getting children and young people involved and literally leaving their mark on the service. It makes a point, too. The resulting acetate is a visual aid throughout the service. It is child-friendly, but it's not too cool for teenagers to colour their thumbs.

Felt-tip pens are passed out, and everyone who wants to then colours their thumb with a pen. They come out to the front to press their thumb onto an acetate leaving their print on it. This is then shown on the overhead projector.

POINT Each thumbprint on the acetate is different. Each of us is made for a unique purpose. In the feeding of the 5,000 Jesus used what people had. The little boy had a packed lunch; the disciples had faith (not much); Jesus could use both. What do you have? What is your unique contribution that Jesus can use?

PREPARATION LEVEL ★ Bring felt-tip pens, making sure they are the sort which will leave an imprint on acetate.

10 VISUAL
Doll with a secret

A simple, all-age illustration. You can ask for volunteers to help you show it off.

Show a Russian doll that contains lots of smaller dolls inside, or one that does an amazing number of things such as speaking, drinking, wetting itself, etc. (If you have someone who is good at origami a variation on this is to use an ordinary sheet of paper that they can use to make into something surprising.)

POINT There is more to this doll (or the sheet of paper) than meets the eye. The same is true for anything and anyone Jesus uses: they have endless possibilities. The boy's packed lunch and the disciples themselves were transformed by Jesus to feed a huge crowd.

PREPARATION LEVEL ★ Get a suitable doll, or origami expert.

11 MIME
Three little posers

Child-friendly. Good for lower (primary) school assemblies.

Three people strike and hold different poses. The first stands with shrugged shoulders; the second holds out their hands as if to push someone away; the third opens their arms as if to embrace someone.

POINT It would have been quite understandable for Jesus not to have cared about the crowd's hunger. He could have felt it was none of his business (point to actor 1) – it was up to them to feed themselves. He was tired – he had been teaching them and healing their sick, so he might have wanted them to go (point to actor 2). But instead he had compassion on them (Matthew 14:14, point to actor 3). Nearly all Jesus' signs were motivated by this same love of God.

PREPARATION LEVEL ★ or ★★ Actors could be found on the spur of the moment but it would help if you knew they could stand still without giggling!

12 DRAMA
Nice rolls

See *Nice Rolls* **(Preparation level ★★★)** on page 41.

THE RAISING OF LAZARUS

Reading: John 11:32-44
Title: 'Dying to live'
'Dead man walking'
'They thought it was all over'

13 STARTER
Happy pictures

Put pictures of smiling, happy people around the church, or a big smile on the OHP.

POINT 'Don't worry, be happy' doesn't work as a philosophy for life. We may feel forced to smile our way through life, but the raising of Lazarus shows that Jesus didn't. As a miracle preparing for the resurrection of Jesus himself, it shows that Jesus looks at death squarely in all the emptiness and the grief it causes ('Jesus wept', verse 35), yet still overcomes it.

PREPARATION LEVEL ★★ Get volunteers to cut out and hang up the pictures.

14 STARTER
No entry

Death is obviously a sensitive subject, but it can be brought up with any age. However, be aware that someone in the congregation might be in the process of mourning.

Put a picture of a 'No Entry' sign on the OHP, or place one at the front of the church.

POINT Death is a sad thing, a tragic thing, a taboo subject. Sometimes it seems as if there is a 'No Entry' sign in our mind to stop us thinking about it. But Jesus didn't look at death like this. He knew that before the joy of resurrection there had to be the pain of death.

PREPARATION LEVEL ★★ Make a sign big enough to be seen from the back of church.

15 VISUAL
Happy ending

The idea of happy endings is familiar to all ages. As with most video clips, this is teenager-friendly. Even children's videos like this can work well.

Show the ending of a film such as *Beauty and the Beast*. The dead beast is brought back to life, transformed into a prince, and the couple live happily ever after.

POINT We love happy endings, and Disney makes sure we get one. But the Lazarus story is not like this. It has a sad beginning as the sisters suffer agonies waiting for Jesus to arrive; a sad middle, as Jesus openly cries for his dead friend; even a sad ending since this sign leads to the Pharisees plotting Jesus' death. However, there is happiness for the relatives of Lazarus, and there is hope for those who trust in Jesus' claim to be the resurrection and the life.

PREPARATION LEVEL ★ ★ ★ You must have a video projector, or someone expert enough to wire up enough TVs to a video recorder for everyone to see – and access to enough TVs.

16 VISUAL
Sports clip

An alternative to the above, for teenagers and older.

Get some footage of the last Boat Race, or of a running race or any endurance event from television.

POINT Stop the video before the final victory, showing the strain on the athletes' faces. Make the point that they keep going although the pain is terrible and one half of them wants to stop. Without death there can be no resurrection, or as the sports coaches put it, 'There's no gain without pain.'

PREPARATION LEVEL ★ ★ ★ You must have a video projector, unless you have someone expert enough to wire up enough TVs to a video recorder for everyone to see – and access to enough TVs.

17 ACTION
Off their marbles

Good for audiences of mixed ages.

A seven-year-old, a teenager and an adult are each given two bags of marbles. The seven-year-old must add together the marbles in each bag; the teenager must subtract the number in one bag from the number in the other; the adult must divide the number in one bag by the number in the other, and then multiply the result by pi, using a calculator. (You need to keep talking while they do this.) An alternative could be to put three mathematical problems of varying degrees of difficulty on the Service Sheet, and take a 'time-out' for people to try and crack them.

POINT Some questions are easier to answer than others. It's easy to think that if we had the brains (such as our three mathematicians), the equipment (such as the calculator) and the inside information (such as the fact that pi is 3.14159), we could work out any question. But this is not so. There are no black and white answers to rainbow-coloured questions such as: Why do we suffer? Why must people die? Why do we have to cry? What we can say is that Jesus went through all of these experiences. He offers no way of escape from them, but he does promise victory and eternal life after death.

PREPARATION LEVEL ★ Prepare suitable bags of marbles. Volunteers could be primed before the service or on the spur of the moment (make sure they don't mind maths!).

18 ACTION
Hanging on

Works best in a family service with a well-known dad and his child.

A child and his/her father are needed as volunteers. The child stands on a stool to take hold of dad's outstretched arms. The stool is then taken away so the child is left dangling in the air. Eventually they will fall the few inches to the floor. Dad picks them up and holds them.

POINT Sometimes it feels as if we have a firm grip on God. We know he loves us and our faith is strong. But then something happens that knocks the ground from under our feet. We find ourselves clinging on to faith by our finger-tips, like our young volunteer. That was how Mary and Martha felt. Perhaps they felt they had lost touch with God, that he had left them, that he had allowed their brother to die. But then they experienced him reaching down to pick them up again.

PREPARATION LEVEL ★★ Get your two volunteers to practise this beforehand with the person who takes the stool away.

19 ACTION
DNA game

Good fun, possibility for movement and all-age involvement.

One side of the church has a large 'D' hanging up, the other side has a large 'A'. People go to one side or the other depending on whether they think what you hold up is Dead/Dying (D) or Alive (A). (Hence the name DNA game.) More sedentary people are allowed to sit where they are and point to whatever they think is the correct answer. You present a seed, a conker, a moving toy, a plant-cutting, a bouquet of flowers, or similar objects you can easily get.

POINT Some things look dead, like a seed or a plant-cutting. But given the right treatment (good soil) they come to life. Other things look alive: the bouquet, for example, looks wonderful but it is dying. The toy moves, but it's just a toy. Jesus can bring new life out of what was dead.

PREPARATION LEVEL ★ Prepare and hang up a large 'D' and 'A', and collect props.

20 ATTENTION GRABBER
Get knotted

Very flexible illustration for all ages. Especially useful in secondary school assemblies when the notices have gone on too long, and the head informs you that your ten-minute slot is now down to two minutes.

Give any number of volunteers a piece of string about 1 metre long. Tell them they are to take the string into both hands and tie a knot in it without letting go of either end. This is impossible unless you start with your arms folded and then take hold of the string. As you unfold your arms, you make a knot.

POINT How you understand the raising of Lazarus depends on your starting-point. If your starting-point is that Jesus was a good man, a great teacher, or just a prophet, the resurrection of Lazarus or indeed anyone is unbelievable. Every miracle is as impossible as tying a knot if your starting point is wrong. But if your starting-point is that Jesus is God, the creator of all life, it would be surprising if he could not bring the dead to life.

PREPARATION LEVEL ★ It doesn't take long to cut up pieces of string or wool.

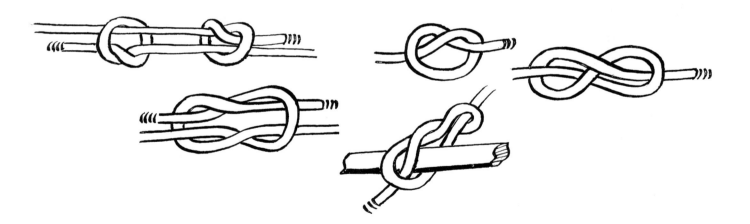

CLOSE ENCOUNTERS

JESUS AND NICODEMUS

📖 **Reading:** John 3:1-8
Title: 'The missing peace'
'Starting again'

21 ↘ STARTER
Jigsaws

Can be used for all ages. Good for creating interest at the beginning of a service and for getting movement in it.

From the moment they come into church, children are invited to do jigsaw puzzles at the front. Or, each child is given a puzzle piece when they arrive, and during the service they come to the front to make the puzzle. The puzzle can also be made on the OHP screen (with supervision) while you are speaking, so everyone sees the pieces being put together.

POINT Whatever age we are, it's natural to want to work out puzzles. One puzzle is the universal human desire for God. C S Lewis wrote, 'If I find in myself a desire which no experience in this world can satisfy, the most probable explanation is that I was made for another world.' This is a puzzle. Nicodemus was puzzled by Jesus, and he wanted an answer.

PREPARATION LEVEL ★ Have puzzles ready at the front of church. For the alternative, have a puzzle with about the same number of pieces as there are likely to be children in church.

22 👍 ACTION
Common idea

For all ages; teenager-friendly. Good for breaking up a service and getting participation.

At the end of each pew or row there is an envelope. The person nearest to it is told to open it, look at the picture or headline in it, and pass it on. It is then passed to another row (or you can get people to shout out what it is and write them up on the OHP); if you pass them round church have a game plan to avoid one row getting ten and another getting none! The aim is for the congregation to guess what the items have in common. The answer is that they are all to do with keeping or getting 'the body beautiful'. The headlines and adverts are about sportspeople or models, getting slimmer, wearing the right clothes, and having the right smell.

POINT Today we spend millions of pounds and hours looking after our bodies. They are important. Yet very little attention is paid to the one part of us that will not shrivel and die.

PREPARATION LEVEL ★★ Find and cut out from newspapers and magazines enough headlines and adverts and pictures to put in envelopes so that you have one for each row of church.

23 👍 ACTION
Find the pieces

Good when young children are present as they are going to be your volunteers. They love a good treasure-hunt.

Children search for the pieces of a ten-piece puzzle. They put the puzzle together on the OHP screen. Nine of the pieces are in obvious places around the church. But one piece is missing.

POINT Imagine buying a new puzzle and one piece is missing. What can you do? You could search for it; you could try and make your own; you could write to the maker and ask for the missing piece. Nicodemus knows something is missing from the puzzle of his life. Without fully realizing what he is doing, he is contacting his Maker when he goes to see Jesus one night.

PREPARATION LEVEL ★ Hide puzzle pieces around the church.

24 ACTION
Knotty problem

Good for young people in uniformed organizations who can be interviewed about the different knots they can tie.

Have some ropes prepared with knots in them. Volunteers have to try to undo the knots. One pair are told to try to undo their knot by pulling as hard as they can on either end.

POINT If you want to undo knots, it helps to know how they were tied in the first place. Our lives sometimes seem as if they are in knots. If we are going to untangle them it is good to know how we were put together. We were designed to know God and be filled with his Spirit. Otherwise we can be like the tug-of-war duo, pulling hard but succeeding only in making the knot tighter. Nicodemus has done well in life, but there is a knot in his life that he can't seem to untie. Only the Holy Spirit can do that for him.

PREPARATION LEVEL ★ Get some ropes and tie knots in them. These can be used solely as a visual aid, or with volunteers trying to undo them.

25 VISUAL
Loose ends

Any age from middle school (9-13) upwards can relate to the fact that each of us is different outside to what we are inside. This is teenager-friendly, and good for secondary school assemblies (wear the jersey).

A hand-knitted jersey looks good on the outside. But if you turn it inside out there are lots of loose ends. On that side it all looks a bit of a mess.

POINT Like this jersey, Nicodemus – and perhaps you too – seems pretty neat on the outside, but has lots of hidden loose ends on the inside. Jesus is always more interested in these loose ends than the image we show on the outside.

PREPARATION LEVEL ★ Find a suitable jersey. If necessary, add loose ends of wool inside!

26 ACTION
Guess who?

Like most games, this brings good fun, involvement and movement. Good for events where no one will be offended at the chaos likely to ensue (so may not be good for all church services). Great for youth weekends away.

Hang around church (or put onto acetate) photos of well-known church members when they were babies or very young. People have to guess who they are.

POINT There is a likeness between a baby and the adult they grow into, if not on the outside then certainly on the inside. The baby's life is spent growing up into that person.

There is also a likeness between ourselves and God. To be 'born again' means the Holy Spirit helps us to grow more like Jesus. Who are you going to grow up becoming like?

PREPARATION LEVEL ★★ Obtain photos of church members as babies or young children, and get permission to use them in this way.

27 QUIZ
Who's the man who can?

For mixed-age audience. Questions are for children, but the teaching point is for all ages.

- If your car broke down, who would you take it to?
- If the computer you had just bought would not work, where would you take it to?
- If you had a tax problem, who would you go to?
- If your pet became ill, who would you see?

POINT When we need something, we go to the right person. That's what Nicodemus did. He was quite embarrassed to do that (he went to Jesus at night). We can all be like that; we don't want to admit we need Jesus.

PREPARATION LEVEL ★ These questions are asked on the spur of the moment, but only to a congregation that is not going to be utterly fazed by this sort of repartee.

28 DRAMA

See 'High Hopes' on page 36.

JESUS AND ZACCHAEUS

 Reading: Luke 19:1-10
Title: 'On the fence up a tree'
'The guest of a sinner'

29 ACTION
Chinese whispers

Teenager-friendly, good for youth events. You need to fill in while the whisper is going down the line.

Play Chinese whispers with a row of young people you have primed beforehand, checking that the first person you give the verse to can read. The verse is Luke 19:10: 'For the Son of man came to seek and to save what was lost.'

POINT Down the centuries the original message of Jesus has been distorted. Today some people think he said, 'People who need help should be ashamed of themselves. I have come to call successful and respectable people.' In fact there are only two sorts of people. There are people who are lost and have been found by Jesus, and people who are lost and who have not been found by him. In Jericho that day, Jesus left the crowds of respectable people, risked his own reputation, and spent the day with a 'lost' person, the black sheep of the town.

PREPARATION LEVEL ★★ Find the volunteers beforehand.

30 VISUAL
Mirror image

Can be used as a visual aid for all ages.

Have a large mirror to show. Use a mirror with its back like the back of a picture, if possible, so that what it is isn't obvious.

POINT Hold the mirror towards you and say you have a picture of someone like Zacchaeus. Just like Zacchaeus this person needs to hear Jesus calling him by name; just like Zacchaeus Jesus wants to spend the day with them in their house, and Jesus also wants to make a difference to them just as he did to Zacchaeus. (Turn the mirror round.) This is the picture. Just as Zacchaeus came down from the tree, so we have to respond to Jesus, and through him see the sort of people we could become.

PREPARATION LEVEL ★ Get a mirror and practise how you will use it.

31 ACTION
Ice age

Good for all ages. Be prepared for a mess, so have towels placed strategically.

Volunteers try to melt a large block of ice. The ice could be used just as a visual aid; you could have lots of small ice-cubes for greater participation.

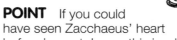

POINT If you could have seen Zacchaeus' heart before he met Jesus, this is what it would have looked like: cold and hard. No amount of effort or force from other people could have changed it. The warmth of God's love and mercy were needed to melt it. When it melted, the whole of Jericho was flooded with joy. Who needed a building society, when there was Zacchaeus to give you a windfall worth four times what he'd taken?

PREPARATION LEVEL ★ Put a bowl of water in a freezer overnight, and bring it to church in an ice-box.

32 VISUAL
Who's the greatest?

For middle school age (9-13) upwards. In schools, the point could be linked to an anti-bully policy if there is one (liaise with staff first).

Volunteers stand on a platform similar to that used for the Olympic Games' medal ceremonies. Give them imaginary or real medals for imaginary or real feats. A simple medal presented to one person will put across the same point.

POINT Someone has called human beings the 'comparing creatures'. We love league tables, medal ceremonies, working out who is better than who. Even the disciples argued among themselves about who would be the greatest (Luke 9:46;22:24). Everyone in Jericho thought they were better than that swindler, fraud, traitor and all-round bad bloke, 'Shorty' Zacchaeus. But Jesus threw away their league tables and showed them that God's mercy is free for anyone.

PREPARATION LEVEL ★

33 STORY

See 'Loan-Shark Larry' on page 27 for a re-telling of the Zacchaeus story.

JESUS AND BARTIMAEUS

Reading: Mark 10:46-52
Title: 'Help! I need somebody!'
'Be quiet, Bartimaeus!'

34 ⬇ STARTER
Tramp in

Can be very effective at youth services and events, but probably not to be used at other church services. You need a good actor who can stay in role no matter what happens.

A dishevelled-looking man is sitting by the church door as people come in. His clothes are not the best, he is staring down at the ground, and there is a plate in front of him. Ideally he is someone unknown to anyone in the congregation, or else he is very well disguised.

POINT How do we react to a stranger, down on their luck, begging? Our reaction may well be that we wish they weren't there, they are an uncomfortable sight, an embarrassing one. It's probably their own fault that they're like that; why don't they go away? That's how the people of Jericho felt about Bartimaeus.

PREPARATION LEVEL ★ Make sure you have the right person for this role.

35 ❓ QUIZ
Close encounters

Idea suitable for any occasion where you can expect feedback: assemblies, church services of any kind, youth events. It can be very good to ask questions to which there is no 'correct answer', but which ask for opinions or experiences.

Ask who has met a famous person. Who was it and what did they say? This can be very interesting and even funny.

POINT In most such encounters the famous person will not have spent a lot of time with you. They had too many places to go to and more people to see, so all they could give you was a brief word, a glance and – if you were lucky – an autograph. But Bartimaeus stopped the Son of God in his tracks. His shouting and crying were very embarrassing for Jesus' fan-club who had turned out to see him. But Jesus, who had come to seek and to save lost people, had time for him.

PREPARATION LEVEL ★ If you are unsure of getting a response, you could prime two or three people beforehand.

36 👓 VISUAL
Dress to tell

Good for secondary school assemblies, youth events. Beware of the strip-tease version for church services where it could offend someone!

You need different layers of clothes to illustrate some of the roles you play in life. For example, a tracksuit top (if you're a sportsperson of any kind), a clerical shirt (if you're ordained), a shirt and tie or formal blouse (for work perhaps), your favourite jersey (you at home), a football shirt (if you support a team). Either put them on in advance and take them off one by one as you talk, or have them in a pile and put them on as you talk, over each other.

POINT All these clothes reflect 'me'. They are an image I want to put across in different situations. But they can all hide the real me, the me who is hurting, the me who is lost, the me who Jesus came to seek. Bartimaeus didn't have any image – what you saw was who he was. It's one reason why Jesus could respond to him and to his need.

PREPARATION LEVEL ★ Get the clothes ready.

37 MIME
Waiting time

Use at secondary schools, youth services, church services. Avoid in primary schools.

Three actors stand in a pose. One is hitch-hiking; one is standing in a queue (have a sign with 'Q here' on it); the third is on the phone.

POINT To wait for someone or something is a dreaded experience. We feel out of control, reliant on other people – like the hitch-hiker who must wait for someone to give him a lift; like the person in the queue who must wait for their turn; like the one on the telephone, waiting for the operator to connect him. All these experiences teach us a truth about life: we are not in control. Bartimaeus had been waiting all his life. He knew he needed help. He was not embarrassed to shout loudly for Jesus. He had nothing to lose.

PREPARATION LEVEL ★ Find three actors.

JESUS AND THE FIRST DISCIPLES

 Reading: Luke 5:1-11 and/or 5:27-32
Title: 'Follow your leader!'
'Fishermen with a new line.'

38 STARTER
Music impossible

Has to be used in a setting where playing this sort of music is acceptable, and where a majority will know of Mission Impossible, *the programme or the film.*

Play theme music from the programme *Mission Impossible*.

POINT *Mission Impossible* was the programme where an amazing team of crime-busters were given a crazy mission on a tape that self-destructed. Because of their great skills, they always succeeded and never destroyed themselves. If Jesus had told the disciples to be 'fishers of men' on their own, it would have been a mission impossible. They did not have it in them. But this was not a mission; it was rather a commission. They would be going with Jesus. By following him, it would be possible.

PREPARATION LEVEL ★★ Find the music and tape it, or get someone to play it well on a keyboard.

39 ACTION
Simon says

Flexible illustration which can be used in different settings, but you have to adapt the Teaching Point for each. You can ask the children to come up to the front and play it with just them.

Play 'Simon says' with as many of the congregation as want to join in. This could be the introduction to the sketch 'Simon says' (page 35) or the story 'Follow me' (page 30). Or, after a couple of rounds, make the teaching point.

POINT In the game you do what Simon says. If he doesn't say it, you don't do it. But who is the Simon in your life, who do you follow? Your boss? Your peer group? The adverts? The latest craze? Your favourite pop-star or film-star? Jesus says, 'Follow me', but you choose whether to or not. The first disciples chose to follow what Jesus said.

PREPARATION LEVEL ★ Gets everyone involved but needs no preparation.

40 MIME
Fishy business

Works well in settings where there is some knowledge of the original Bible story (i.e. when it has already been read in the service) and when you have a good volunteer. There is a danger of the illustration masking the message.

Get a volunteer (primed beforehand) to do some fishing at the front of church, or have them doing so at the church door when people enter. Ask them throughout the talk whether they have caught anything, and whether they believe they'll catch anything, then ask them why they're continuing to fish.

POINT Simon, like our volunteer fisherman, hadn't caught anything all night; like our fisherman here he didn't believe he would catch anything; the only reason he went out into the lake again was because Jesus had told him to. (At this point you could have someone hook a packet of fish-fingers or a kipper onto the fishing-line, and get your fisherman to wind it in.) It takes a miracle to catch something here!

PREPARATION LEVEL ★★ Get fishing tackle; prime volunteers including one to hook on the fish if you plan to use this part.

41 QUIZ
Answer please

Good in evangelistic settings. Care needs to be taken with the teaching point in schools where direct evangelism is not allowed.

What are the four letters you find at the bottom of an invitation? Clue: we're not looking here for the answer F-R-O-M. Get volunteers to hold up R-S-V-P.

POINT When Jesus said, 'Follow me', it wasn't an order. Any of the disciples could have said, 'No.' They could have said and done nothing, gone their own way. It was an invitation, and like all the invitations it had the letters R-S-V-P coming after it. By leaving everything and following Jesus, they made it clear what their reply was.

PREPARATION LEVEL ★ Make letters in A4 size.

42 VISUAL
Heavy work

No good in primary schools as children shouldn't lift weights. Could be used in a secondary school, getting the school strongman to help you after you've failed to lift the weight on your own; also in services with a primed volunteer.

You have at the front a weight-training bar with weights on. Either you or a primed volunteer tries to lift the weights, but cannot do so. (Take care with this if you have not had any training, as it is possible to put your back out: weights must be lifted with knees bent. In any case you or the volunteer should pretend not to be able to lift the weight.) It takes someone else at the other end to help you lift the bar.

POINT Simon understands that Jesus is calling him to do things he could not possibly do on his own. His reaction, 'I am a sinful man', shows how over-awed he is by what has just happened. The amazing catch of fish was a sign for him of what he could do if he followed Jesus and drew on Jesus' power.

PREPARATION LEVEL ★★ You will need to carry a heavy weight to the location of your talk; you also need to get a volunteer to help with the illustration.

STORY-TIMES

THE PARABLE OF THE TALENTS

📖 **Reading:** Matthew 25:14-30 *(see dramatic reading 'Talented' on page 40 for one way to present this)*
Title: 'Talented!'
'Don't bury it!'
'Unwrap your gift!'

43 ↘ STARTER
Gifts wrapped

Good for all settings where you can get volunteers to come up.

Have the following 'gifts' wrapped up: a saw (with a safety-cover on it), a pair of knitting needles, an artist's paint-brush, a pen, a tennis-racket, a cooking spoon, or whatever you have which will make the same point. Invite some volunteers to unwrap them. Ask what all the gifts have in common.

POINT Simply, they all represent gifts people have. Everyone has at least one gift, or talent. Some people are born talented at carpentry, knitting, painting, writing, tennis, cooking. But we each have to 'unwrap', or discover what it is. No baby is born with a label stuck on it saying 'star tennis-player', 'brilliant writer', or 'great cook'. Everyone has to work to find out their gift, and then use it. The problem with the final servant in the reading was that he did nothing with the gift he had been given.

PREPARATION LEVEL ★★ Wrap up gifts beforehand.

44 👓 VISUAL
Mystery gift

Can be used in every setting.

You give a wrapped parcel to someone (who has been primed) in the congregation. They act as though they are delighted, ecstatic, and generally overwhelmed by your generosity. You wait for them to unwrap it, but they don't want to. As an alternative, you could describe someone getting this parcel and never opening it. The parcel stays in a prominent place throughout the service as a constant reminder of what the theme is. At the end it is opened to reveal a packet of sunflower seeds. A young person gives one to each person as they leave the service as a reminder that everyone has been given something; it's up to them what they do with it.

POINT Imagine getting a gift, and never finding out what's inside, just admiring the wrapping paper. Yet that's what many people do with what God has given them.

PREPARATION LEVEL ★ Wrap up one box large enough to be seen by everyone, with sunflower seeds inside.

45 👓 VISUAL
Book back

Best used with adults. It's only an analogy and can't be pushed too far.

Hold up a library book.

POINT This book does not belong to you. If you keep hold of it too long, you have to pay a fine. It's the same with the talents each of the servants had. Two of them remembered that their talents were not their own but had to be returned well looked-after to the owner at the due time. None of our talents are our own, we have them from our Maker. We have to give an account for them to him.

PREPARATION LEVEL ★ Get a library book.

46 ❓ QUIZ
Who's afraid?

Can be used in all settings. In primary schools needs to be combined with how Jesus helps us in our fears. It's important – and perhaps obvious – not to make fun of phobias, as they can ruin some people's lives.

Put four pictures on an OHP acetate: a spider, an aeroplane, a mountain, and darkness (cover each picture with a piece of paper until you mention it). What do they all have in common? They are all common phobias: many people are afraid of spiders, of flying, of heights and of the dark.

POINT There is one thing probably everyone is afraid of: failure. That's what paralyzed the third servant. It was because he was afraid that he did nothing with what the king had given him. The life of faith to which Jesus invites his followers is the opposite of this paralyzing fear.

PREPARATION LEVEL ★★ You probably need some computer technology to get this acetate done, or a willing volunteer to do it for you. Otherwise you could use a plastic spider, a model aeroplane, someone standing on a chair and a blindfold to represent the four fears.

47 👓 VISUAL
Different jobs

Works with an audience familiar with DIY, but not in primary schools. Please be careful how you use the words 'tool' and 'screw'. If you don't know why, make sure you get all your talks checked for words with double meanings by someone who's worldly-wise.

A tool-box. Inside is a claw hammer, a Swiss army knife, a screwdriver.

POINT The knife is designed to do many things; the hammer can do two things (bang in nails and lift them out again); the screwdriver is for just one thing, to put in screws. Everyone here has a different number of talents. Swiss army knives are different to screwdrivers. To get a job done, you need everything in the tool-box. In the same way, God needs everyone to use their talents. Often people with single talents don't use theirs, perhaps because they think they're not as talented and therefore not as essential as others.

PREPARATION LEVEL ★ Find a tool-box with what you need inside.

48 ☺ DRAMA

See *The World's Greatest Athlete* on page 34.

THE PARABLE OF THE RICH FOOL

📖 **Reading:** Luke 12:13-21.
   Title: 'Wrong way!'
          'A wasted life'
          'You fool!'

49 👍 ACTION
Ad mission

Can be used with audiences who have some awareness of advertising. Teenager-friendly.

Put into envelopes a selection of adverts cut from magazines. Stick the envelopes on the ends of pews or under chairs. At a given moment everyone looks for an envelope, looks at what's inside, then passes it down the row. Get people to raise their hands to find out who was encouraged by which advert to consider buying the product.

POINT All sorts of things look very attractive. The adverts play on this fact. Sometimes they make us feel that if we don't have this product we're not living. Jesus taught that life is not about possessions. The rich fool's mistake was to think that if he owned enough, he'd have 'made it'.

PREPARATION LEVEL ★★ It takes some time to find suitable ads, cut them out, put them in envelopes and then place the envelopes in church.

50 VISUAL
Dream products

Good for any audience where materialism is likely to be an issue.

As an alternative to no. 49, have on show a bottle of after-shave; a packet of soap powder; a can of Coke; a pair of running shoes.

POINT You bought all of these because you believed the adverts. They told you that if you had this smell you'd be irresistible; that your clothes would be whiter than white; that 'things would go better' if you drank this; and you'd become a star-athlete if you wore these. They've all been rather disappointing. None of the dreams that were sold with these things have come true. No one thing and no amount of things will ever truly satisfy. Even if our dreams were fulfilled, we'd still want more.

The rich man was a fool to believe that he could buy himself a life of ease.

PREPARATION LEVEL ★ Bring along a number of items you've seen advertised.

51 MIME
Single mind

Works where people are likely to have some interest in or awareness of sport.

An actor mimes the focused look of an athlete like Linford Christie at the start of his races, who stared down his running lane to the finish, not letting anything or anyone distract him from his aim. This will have more effect if there are obvious distractions. (Or you could use a video clip of Linford Christie's famous stare.)

POINT What are you focused on? Perhaps it's whatever or whoever your mind dwells on when you're day-dreaming. An athlete like Linford Christie focuses only on one thing: the finish-line. The rich fool was focused on getting as much wealth as he could.

PREPARATION LEVEL ★ Find someone to do the mime well.

52 VISUAL
Date control

Best used in a church setting. It is meant to make people think that you're going to talk about the Bible.

Hold up your diary.

POINT In your hand you have one of the world's best-selling books. Most people have at least one, many of you would say you'd never leave home without it; you look in it daily and let it guide your life. Yes, a diary is very important, perhaps because it gives the illusion that we are in control of our lives. Yet we all know that many things happen to us that were never written in it. The rich fool was a fool not because he was rich, but because he thought his riches would put him in control. But he was wrong.

PREPARATION LEVEL ★ Just take your diary to the meeting.

53 VISUAL
Robin red-face

Excellent visual aid when teenagers and/or adults are present if the technology (video projector, recorder, screen, black-out) is available.

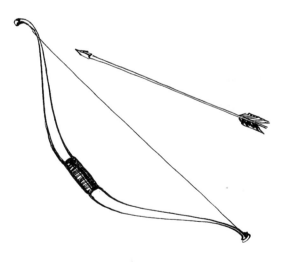

Show a clip from the film *Robin Hood, Prince of Thieves*. Robin is showing off his prowess at archery to his merry men, but as he concentrates on the target, Maid Marion distracts him so he misses by a mile.

POINT God has given us a target to aim at: to love him with all our heart and mind and soul and strength; in other words to be rich towards him (verse 21). But we are distracted from his target by many things.

PREPARATION LEVEL ★ ★ ★ Get the equipment in place.

THE PARABLE OF THE MERCILESS SERVANT

📖 **Reading:** Matthew 18:21-35
Title: 'Pass it on!'

54 ❓ QUIZ

Can be adapted for different audiences. Good for general participation, fun, with a sting in the tail.

The congregation have to complete the following sentences or any other well-known slogan, sentence or line of a song:
- Baa baa black sheep … *(have you any wool?)*.
- Twinkle, twinkle … *(little star)*.
- Oooo aaaaa … *(Cantona)*.
- Every little … *(helps)*.
- Vorsprung durch … *(Technik)*.

POINT Certain phrases roll off the tongue because we have heard them so often and we know them by heart. Here is a longer one: Forgive us our sins … (as we forgive those who sin against us). It's easy to say that. Have you ever thought about what it means? The character in our reading never had. In praying it, we are asking God to forgive us in the same way that we forgive others. It's a prayer he answers, perhaps in an uncomfortable way, as our reading shows.

PREPARATION LEVEL ★ Think through what catch-phrases and sentences are known well enough by most of the audience/congregation.

55 👍 ACTION
Blocked tubes

Good to get older volunteers for the pouring, ideally done on staging where the exercise is visible. Should be fun.

You need pieces of tubing, preferably transparent and at least one metre in length. Taking great care not to get everything soaked, a volunteer pours water into one end. Another volunteer holds a bowl at the other end. One piece of tubing has a marble or something similar stuck in it (this can be pushed in by a long knitting needle). The water obviously will not flow through it.

POINT God gives us his gifts with the intention that we use them and pass them on. His forgiveness, his Holy Spirit, his love are all meant to be received, and then overflow from us. The unmerciful servant is like the tube that is bunged up; he wanted to keep the forgiveness he'd received for himself. It made no difference at all to the way he thought about others (verse 33), so he lost everything he had received.

PREPARATION LEVEL ★★ Get all the materials you need in place, including towels, and prime volunteers for the pouring.

56 👓 VISUAL
Pass it on

Easy to understand as long as people know the concept of a relay race.

You need a relay baton. As an alternative you could use the collection plate or a collection bag in church. Again, the idea is that it has to be handed on otherwise you would be punished as a thief.

POINT The baton in a relay race has to be handed on from one runner to another, otherwise the race is lost or the team disqualified. In the same way, the forgiveness of God has to be handed on. It is a free gift, a sign of God's incredible mercy; but if it is misused, it becomes evidence against us.

PREPARATION LEVEL ★ Find a relay baton or use the collection plate.

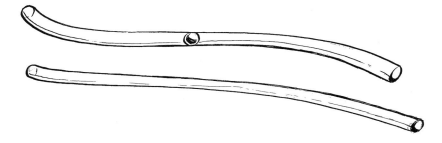

57 VISUAL
Sand wit

Can be used with or without a volunteer, with a point that should be grasped or at least sensed by every age group.

Hold up a bucket of sand. Ask a volunteer to come out to illustrate what it's like to try and earn God's forgiveness. What we'd like you to do is… count how many grains of sand there are in this bucket.

POINT The servant told the king, 'I will pay back everything.' Some hope! He might just as well have promised to count the grains of sand here. It was an impossible task – he owed the salary he earned thousands and thousands of times over.

It's a picture of how immense and endless is the forgiveness of God. When Jesus tells Peter he should forgive seventy-seven times, he's really saying that forgiveness can never end.

PREPARATION LEVEL ★ Bring along a bucket of sand.

58 DRAMA

See *I'll buy it!* on page 32. It links with the point that the unforgiving servant thought that he would be able to pay back the king and earn his forgiveness. See also *The Servant Who Didn't Forgive* on page 31.

PART TWO

TELL US A STORY!
STORIES AND SKETCHES

Stories and sketches can be wonderful; they can also be naff. What they should be doing is making us curious, telling us something familiar enough to be believable but dramatic enough to be interesting. When they touch our imagination, make us wonder 'What will happen next?', and surprise us with an odd twist or two, they have worked. They may also leave us wondering, 'What was that about?' That is what Jesus' listeners often asked at the end of a parable. But they had been captivated enough to seek out the answer for themselves.

When stories start to preach, they overreach themselves and people cringe. It is far better to provoke questions. Most of Jesus' teaching is in response to questions; he didn't force his truth on anyone not interested.

So his parables suggested a great deal, they opened up hearts and minds to possibilities about God, and they set people wondering. Sometimes without mentioning God directly, they said much to people who wanted to find him.

SOME STORIES TO TELL

These need a good story-teller and an audience ready to go along with them.

59 THE TUNE-MAKER

This can be a moving story or sketch for the end of an evening, when you want to say something about God but not too much, and fairly gently. You can use actors miming the different actions whilst the story is being read. This and the co-ordination of the music requires quite a lot of rehearsing.

POINT
'In the past God spoke to our forefathers... in various ways, but in these last days he has spoken to us by his son.' (Hebrews 1:1-2). So listen hard!

PREPARATION LEVEL
★★ With just a good keyboard player and narrator
★★★ When you have actors miming the story as well

(IDEA TAKEN FROM A SONG PERFORMED BY LARRY NORMAN AT A CONCERT IN INNSBRUCK, AUSTRIA, 1988)

'The tune' is playing. This will be an instrumental piece with a simple and recognizable theme that recurs. After a short while the narration starts.

Once upon a time there was a tune-maker. And he composed a tune for the whole world. Every animal and every person knew it by heart. They would wake up in the morning singing it. They would go to sleep humming it. And the strange thing was, it never became boring. The whole world was full of the tune, and the tune-maker was happy.

Until one day *(the tune stops)* somebody thought it could be fun to add a few notes of their own.

(Music restarts with a slight variation, a different key perhaps.)

At first it didn't sound very different. When other people heard it they thought the new tune was marvellous. 'We're sure the tune-maker won't mind,' they said. 'We just want to spice him up a bit.' So they did.

(Music continues to go further and further away from the original tune, growing more and more discordant as the following is read...)

The only trouble was, the new tunes quickly went out of fashion. Everybody had their own favourites. Wars broke out between supporters of different tunes.

(The music ends on a clashing discordant note.)

For hundreds of years nobody heard very much from the old tune-maker. Until one day *(the original tune starts very softly)* a very strange person turned up with his music. He sang it very quietly. Not many people heard it at first: just a few fishermen, a prostitute or two, the odd tax collector.

But they all started to hum the old tune. It was like magic how it spread. Soon thousands of people were coming out to hear how it sounded. They didn't always understand it. But they knew it was something special. They wanted to hear more.

The world's new music industry was furious. *(Rumbling tones played.)* If everyone started singing the old tune, they said, they wouldn't have anything to sell. Record shops would go bust; radios wouldn't be bought; there wouldn't be any charts. One thing was certain – that protégé of the old tune-maker, or whoever he was, would have to go. That would put an end to his music once and for all.

So they crucified him.

(The rumbling stops, and three discordant, loud chords are played.)

And that was that – they thought. The bosses of the music industry held a great party to celebrate their victory. *(Party music is played.)*

Because it was so hot with all the guests, they had to open a window.

And when they did, they heard something very, very frightening from outside. *(The old tune takes over the party music.)* It was the old tune. There was nobody there, you could almost think it was the wind, but no – it was definitely the old tune. Easy to miss; easy to overhear; playing softly, gently, hauntingly in the air. The tune was back. And it has been ever since. So listen hard. *(The tune plays and softly fades.)*

60 LOAN-SHARK LARRY

If you have a good story-teller and can use some local touches for humour, this works in a family service looking at Jesus' encounter with Zacchaeus. You could even tell it instead of the reading.

POINT
We are each in this story. But who? One of the crowd, who thinks the King must be crazy? Larry, who needs a new start in life and gets it? Or one of the great and the good, annoyed at the King's priorities? Jesus wants to have a word with each one, just as he did with Zacchaeus in Jericho some 2,000 years ago.

PREPARATION LEVEL
★★ Needs a good story-teller; it would be great to tell it naturally without a script

Once upon a time, in the future, there was a great stir in the town. The King was coming! Posters said so outside every church. The *(name of local newspaper)* carried banner headlines about it. Everyone was talking about it on *(name of local radio station)*. I'm not surprised: the King had never been here before.

The front gardens along *(name of main road)* were neatly manicured to welcome the King's procession. The '*(name of town)* in bloom' flower-pots were put on every street corner. Shop-windows were polished to a sparkle, the roads were swept dustless. Dignitaries put on their very best attire, and a long, red carpet was unrolled along *(name of the main shopping street)* all the way up to *(name of monument or building at end of the shopping street)*.

There at 11.56 a.m. the King would meet the great and the good of the town. At 12.09 he would open the new Japanese car plant on what used to be *(name of local park)*; at 12.27 he would visit the new BT Internet headquarters where the library had been; at 12.51 he would say good-bye to the mayor. What a day!

The crowds were enormous. Waving, shouting, pushing, shoving, desperate to get a view of the King – and that was just the press. The King was here! The cavalcade of cars with bodyguards running alongside reached the *(name of place on outskirts of town)* at 11.52, the *(name of next place nearer to town-centre)* at 11.54. The great and the good combed their hair, straightened their jackets and dresses, and practised their bows and curtsies.

But what was this? The King's car stopped. Outside 'Larry's Loans'. The dingy place with the sign outside: 'Come to us at your inconvenience'. It had only been open a couple of years, but everyone knew the shark who owned the place. Only a small man, but a giant swindler! Talk was that nasty things could happen if you weren't on time with your repayments.

The King got out of his car, walked through the crowd, and into 'Larry's Loans'. It was 11.55. This shouldn't have been happening. You could see the King through the shop window. He was talking with Larry and his crooked cronies. What was he playing at? Now it was 11.58, and the great and the good were worried. Half an hour went by, and they were distraught. So were the PR people at the Japanese car plant – their engines were overheating. And the net surfers at BT were crashing their mice. Nobody knew what the King was doing.

Nobody except Larry, that is. I must say, the King's visit certainly seemed to do him some good. Talk of the town he was, after that. Especially when he started paying back interest to his old customers. Larry's even given half of everything he owns to charity! Would you believe it?

So that was nice. But it was a strange thing for the King to do: to spend all his time in *(name of town)* with such a bad man. And to ignore the great and the good, the Japanese car makers and the BT Internet surfers. Some said he was right. But most people thought he was crazy. Not least when he said it was people like Larry he'd really come to see.

61 THE LIFEGUARD

Needs a good story-teller, could be used as part of an evening of sketches and readings with music or video clips to follow.

POINT
We tend to blame God whenever things go wrong: 'How could a loving God let this happen to me?' We even do it when we break his rules.

PREPARATION LEVEL
★★ Needs some practice to tell it well

The life-guard was sad. Hardly anyone noticed him or needed him. Except when there was an emergency of course – then everyone called for help. He always came to the rescue. But no one thanked him for it. They just said to each other afterwards: 'Goodness, that was lucky, they could have drowned.'

Some of the children who visited his swimming-pool even made fun of him. 'Look at him sitting on his chair,' they'd say. 'I bet he can't really swim.'

Actually, he could swim. He could have taught them a lot about swimming. But they didn't want to learn. Some of them said, 'That's the kill-joy who won't let us run on the side. He won't let us go in the deep end, we can't dive-bomb our mates, or take lilos in his pool. In fact he won't let us do anything we'd like to.'

The life-guard knew those rules were important. They were there to keep everyone safe. But they didn't want to believe that. Besides, it wasn't all true what they said; the deep-end was only out of bounds once a week, when the diving club was in action.

One Tuesday evening, the divers were there as usual. A rope separated them off from the rest of the pool. But two of the children at the other end had got bored of the shallow end. 'Hey, look at me, Mr Life-Guard! I'm touching the rope!' one said.

'Hey, look at me, Mr Life-Guard! I'm going under the rope!' called the other.

'You keep out of there, sonny!' the life-guard shouted from his high chair. 'It's dangerous!'

'Stuff you, Mr Life-Guard.'

The boy had only just surfaced and got the words out when the diver hit him. Coming from the high board, a double somersault with pike, he had no chance to miss the boy. He struck him a glancing blow on the side of the head and the two of them went down, down, in a fury of bubbles and foam. Down below the surface from where the boy had just come. And where he stayed, motionless, on the bottom of the pool. As the other children and the divers looked on horrified, the life-guard dived in.

It was a close thing. If the life-guard had been a moment or two later, if he hadn't known how to administer artificial resuscitation, if the swimming pool management hadn't phoned so quickly for an ambulance, it might all have been a different story.

As for the boy, he suffered mild concussion and headaches for the next month or so. He's not too worried because his parents may be getting richer. They're suing the life-guard.

'We can't believe a good life-guard could ever let a thing like that happen!' they told everyone who would listen.

RESPONSE STORIES

These are especially good in primary schools or at a holiday club for telling a Bible story and getting maximum involvement. There is a response for everyone to make when certain 'buzz words' in the story are mentioned.

62 'FOLLOW ME'

Could be used in connection with Jesus and the First Disciples on page 18. This mixing of Matthew 4:18-22 with Luke 5:27-28 works well in primary schools. It can be told with children at the front holding up the buzz words in large letters on card at the front; when they hear the word in the story, they turn the card round to show the response that has to be made.

POINT
Jesus is still saying to would-be disciples today, 'Follow me.' What will you have to leave behind?

PREPARATION LEVEL
★
(★★ if you have to make cards)

RESPONSES
- **Disciples** – *Follow me!*
- **Fish** – *What a whopper!* (Hold arms out as fisherman do when describing their latest catch)
- **Tax collector/money** – *Clink, clink, clink* (with hand actions as though counting money)
- **Walking** – *step, step, step* (stamp three times with feet)
- **Nets** – action of throwing out net, then *Splash!*

Once upon a time there were two fishermen: Simon and his brother Andrew. They spent all day dreaming of catching big **fish**. They would say every evening, as they remembered the **fish** – yes it really was a whopper they'd caught that day.

They worked on the Sea of Galilee, casting out their **nets**, and bringing them in to see if they'd caught a **fish**.

One day Jesus was there **walking** along the shore of the Sea of Galilee. He saw the fishermen casting out their **nets**, and catching **fish**. But Jesus knew they could do something better than catch **fish**, however big they were. He wanted Simon and Andrew to be his **disciples**, Jesus said to them.

The two brothers got up from their **nets**, left them there, and went after Jesus who was **walking** further along the shore. Then he saw two other brothers: James and John. They liked to help their father catch **fish**, and when it was, their father was very pleased. Jesus knew these two brothers should also be his **disciples**, he said to them, and James and John got up from their **nets**, and went after Jesus who was **walking** further on.

As they went, they saw a **tax collector** counting his **money**. On and on, counting his **money** all day long. No **nets** to throw out, no **fish** or even tiddlers to catch, just **money** to count.

Jesus knew the **tax collector** could do something better than that. Levi could be his **disciple**. 'Follow me,' he said, so Levi left his **money** for someone else to count, and he started **walking** behind Jesus.

They all found there was something better for them to do than to catch **fish**, yes even those; something better to do than throw out **nets**; there was something better to do than count **money**. They all became Jesus' **disciples**, 'Follow me,' Jesus had said to them, and they all did, and they spent the rest of their lives doing that. **Walking** with Jesus.

63 THE SERVANT WHO DIDN'T FORGIVE

As above, cards can be held at the front with the buzz words on them. Can be used in an informal setting instead of the reading.

POINT
Each of us is like the servant. We have been let off a huge debt by a powerful and loving King. So we face a big question. What is our response to such forgiveness – are we like the unforgiving servant?

PREPARATION LEVEL
★
(★★ if you have to make cards)

Responses
King – *Your Majesty* (and bow)
Pay – *Now* (and hold hand out)
Penniless – *Aaaaaaaa*
Prison – *Save me!*
Everything – *What? Everything?*

Once upon a time there was a servant who served a rich and powerful **king**. 'Your Majesty,' said the servant, as he was called into the throne-room one day.

'You owe me ten thousand talents, and now you must **pay**', said the **King**. 'Your Majesty,' said the servant falling on his knees. 'I can't, I'm **penniless**.

Since he was not able to **pay**, his master ordered that he and his whole family and **everything**, yes, **everything**, be sold to repay the debt.

The servant fell to his knees and cried out, 'Great and glorious **King**, please have pity on me! I'm only a poor, **penniless** servant.' The servant's master felt sorry for him. He decided to let him off **everything**, yes **everything**, he owed and he let him go.

When that servant left the throne-room, he found one of his fellow-servants who owed him a few pence. 'You owe me one hundred denarii, and now you must **pay** me **everything**. Yes, that's right, **everything**.'

His fellow-servant fell on his knees. 'I can't, I'm **penniless**', he said. But that servant he owed the money to would not forgive him. Instead, he went off and had the man thrown into **prison**. 'Save me!' cried the man. But he wouldn't. He was too angry about the few pence he was owed.

But that was nothing compared to the anger of the **King**. 'Your Majesty,' said the servant who wouldn't forgive when he was called back into the throne-room. 'I let you off **everything**,' said the King. 'Yes, the whole of what you owed me. But you wouldn't forgive your fellow-servant who was **penniless** who asked you for mercy.'

In his anger, the **King** threw the servant who wouldn't forgive into **prison**. 'Save me!' he cried, but the jailers tortured him until he should be able to **pay** back **everything**, yes, the whole lot that he owed.

SIMPLE DRAMAS

A simple drama is one that can be done with the minimum of props and rehearsed half an hour before the service or event is due to begin. The words can be either ad-libbed to get across the gist (although the actors have to be able to do this) or else the actors mime, while the story-line is read by narrators who can use scripts. A drama like this, however simple and short, can be a superb 'window' for a point to be made.

64 I'LL BUY IT!

Can be used in the middle of a talk with you, the speaker, playing the part of Pete as you suddenly notice John in the audience and start the sketch with him. This works better than saying: 'And now we have a little drama to show how hard it is to accept the gift of grace.' Can be used with the parable of the unforgiving servant who thought he could earn the king's forgiveness.

CAST
Pete *(or actor's name)*
John *(or actor's name)*

POINT
We can be very bad at accepting free gifts. This goes for God's gifts as well. When it comes to salvation or forgiveness, we like to get them the old-fashioned way. We want to earn them.

PREPARATION LEVEL
★ If you have the right actors. If not, don't even attempt it.

Pete John, have a present.
John Er, but it's not my birthday, Pete. You must have got the wrong date.
Pete I know it's not your birthday. But I saw it in the shop, and thought you'd like it. So I bought it for you.
John You bought it for me? Just like that?
Pete Yeah! Why not?
John Well, that's really amazing of you, Pete. Erm, let me at least pay you for it.
Pete It's a present, for goodness sake. For you.
John Well, at least let me do something for you in return.
Pete But I don't want anything doing.

(They walk off down the centre aisle arguing.)

John I couldn't possibly take it, no Pete, really, I just couldn't.
Pete Go on, take it.

(Continue saying this as they leave.)

65 NO TIME FOR THE PRESENT

An alternative to the above making the same teaching point. It is more involved, but if you have a good drama group it can be done with little rehearsing. This is a flexible sketch. You can use fewer actors than the full cast if necessary, and you can tailor it to your own situation. It is especially useful for Pentecost or for an evangelistic event. The ending is optional. If you include it, there are lines to be learnt. The narrators can read their lines.

CAST *(variable)*
Narrator 1
Narrator 2
Actor 1
Actor 2
Actor 3
Actor 4
Actor 5

POINT
As *'I'll buy it!'* on page 32. Also illustrates the suspicion we have about anything free, unknown and over which we have no control.

PREPARATION LEVEL
★ or ★★ *if you use actors, who need to learn lines*

Narrator 1	Once upon a time there was a present. *(Points to present in centre of stage.)*
Narrator 2	In fact, there still is the same present.
Narrator 1	And lots of people come to look at it. *(Other actors come to look at it, some look inside. They all stand still in different poses looking at it.)*
Narrator 2	It's free.
Narrator 1	Anyone can have it.
Narrator 2	But they weren't sure they wanted it.

The following lines could be said by different actors if they can remember them, or by the narrators in turn as each actor comes forward and mimes instead.

Actor 1	I don't like the wrapping paper. *(Shakes his head.)*
Actor 2	None of my friends are having it. So neither am I.
Actor 3	*(Looks inside.)* It looks a bit old-fashioned to me.
Actor 4	It could be dangerous.
Actor 5	I know other people who've got this. And it's changed their life.
Actor 4	I don't want to change my life.
Actor 3	I'm very happy as I am, thank you.
Actor 2	I want to be like everyone else.
Actor 1	It's probably all a trick.
Narrator 1	So no one took the present. *(Actors fold their arms in a line behind the present.)*
Narrator 2	They didn't know who it was from. *(They all shake their heads.)*
Narrator 1	Whoever it was probably wanted to get their money. *(They all nod their heads.)*
Narrator 2	After all, everyone knows there's no such thing as a free gift these days. *(They all nod again.)*

SKETCH COULD FINISH HERE OR WITH THIS LAST SECTION.

Actor 1	I don't like the wrapping paper.
Narrator 1	God demonstrates his own love for us in this: While we were still sinners, Christ died for us.
Actor 2	None of my friends are having it. So neither am I.
Narrator 2	Jesus said: Follow me, and I will make you fishers of men.
Actor 3	It looks a bit old-fashioned to me.
Narrator 1	Jesus Christ is the same yesterday, today and for ever.
Actor 4	It could be dangerous.
Narrator 2	Jesus said: I have come so that you might have life, and have it to the full.
Actor 5	I know other people who have got this. And it's changed their lives.
Narrator 1	Jesus said: Now this is eternal life – that they may know you, the only true God, and Jesus Christ, whom you have sent.

66 THE WORLD'S GREATEST ATHLETE

Can be used with music playing in the background, even better with video clips shown also on a large screen behind the sketch of runners winning races on the track. Works at youth events and family services equally well. Could be quite poignant.

CAST
Narrator
Actor

POINT
Can be used in conjunction with the Parable of the Talents on page 20. The question is not whether we are talented; everyone is. The question is what we do with what we have.

PREPARATION LEVEL
★ A very simple sketch and easy to act; only use the video if the technology and expertise is available.

While the narrator speaks, the actor is lounging lazily in an armchair, drinking Coke, pretending to watch TV, using the remote-control occasionally, eating chocolates and generally playing the slob.

Narrator She was the world's greatest athlete. Phenomenal acceleration, perfect physique, steady heart beat, exceptional lung capacity and lightning fast reactions made her into a world-record holder for her age and unbeaten in every race she entered ... Sadly, she stopped competing at the age of 14. We never heard of her again.

Actor Who wants to run anyway? It was just too much like hard work.

67 SIMON SAYS...

Flexible sketch. You can use the first part alone to make the point, by playing the game 'Simon says', followed by the interruption from the audience. The mime in the second part needs to be done well by the actors involved, and could be effective for all ages from middle school (9-13) upwards.

CAST
Narrator
Actor

POINT
Can be used in conjunction with Jesus and the First Disciples on page 18. This sketch opens up the issue of peer pressure which operates at all ages, and asks the question: Who are you following? The pressure to conform as opposed to letting oneself be transformed by the Holy Spirit, to follow others rather than Christ, is immense.

PREPARATION LEVEL
★ if just using first part of sketch
★★ for whole thing
Since a number of actors are involved, there does need to be at least one rehearsal beforehand.

Narrator Simon says, will you please sit down. Simon says, scratch your nose. Simon says, stamp your feet. Simon says, stop doing that. Simon says, shake your neighbour's hand. Simon says, put your hands in the air. Simon says, shake them about.

Actor *(from the audience, interrupting)* Excuse me, who's Simon?

Narrator He's the one who tells us what to do.

Actor Who says he does?

Narrator Simon says. He says everything to us. By the way, Simon says, you can stop shaking your hands in the air now.

The sketch now continues with this mime:

Actor comes on, reading. Stands centre stage, still reading. A group of two or three come on, look at actor reading, point at her and laugh, making fun of her. One goes over to her, snatches the book, looks at the title, and doubles up laughing. Goes over to others, points to reader, and they laugh still more. Reader stops. Looks at them all. Wonders what to do, then puts book down, and goes over to them. They go over to book on ground, and kick it around, before going off leaving her alone. She hesitates. Then she kicks the book, and goes off in their direction.

Narrator Do not conform.

Same actor as above comes on playing flute or recorder (mimed), with actual music being played on keyboard. Group come on as above, playing guitars (mimed). They stop and look at the flute-player. As above, they laugh at her, point to her, and make fun of her. As above, she puts down the imaginary flute, and goes over to them. They all go off playing guitars.

Narrator Do not conform any longer to the pattern of this world.

Actor comes on, stands as though waiting for bus. Others come on, all wearing baseball caps. As above, they laugh at her. She wonders what is wrong this time, then realizes she doesn't have the necessary cap. Goes to audience, miming that she wants a cap. Pays someone for a cap, then is accepted. They all go off together.

Narrator Do not conform any longer to the pattern of this world, but be transformed by the renewing of your mind.

Three people come on carrying signs: Don't touch! Don't look! Don't listen! The group come on as before and laugh at the signs. They touch, look and listen deliberately at each of the signs and laugh while doing so. The actor comes on as above. They try to get her to join them. She wonders what to do. Everyone freezes in their position.

Narrator Do not conform any longer to the pattern of this world, but be transformed by the renewing of your mind. Then you will be able to test and approve what God's will is – his good, pleasing and perfect will. Romans, chapter twelve, verse two.

68 HIGH HOPES

Short and sweet, easy to do, this sketch can be linked with Jesus and Nicodemus or the parable of the rich fool.

CAST
Actor 1
Actor 2
Actor 3

POINT
Suppose we were to become really fit and make the team; look really good and find the perfect partner; pass all our exams and get on in life. These would all be great successes, they would certainly make us happy – for a while. But would they be enough? We are more than just a body, a mind, and a bunch of emotions.

PREPARATION LEVEL
★ Three actors who would need one quick rehearsal

Three actors with their backs to the audience each turn round one after the other.

Actor 1 *(Turns round, starts lifting dumb-bells.)* Just fifteen minutes' more weights. I really hope I make the team on Saturday.

Actor 2 *(Turns round, doing tie in mirror.)* I wonder which jacket goes with this tie? Do you think she'll like it? I really hope she wants to go out with me.

Actor 3 *(Turns round, reading a book.)* 'After a modal verb, the infinitive goes at the end of the sentence.' Oh, I really hope I pass this German exam.

They all freeze in position.

DRAMAS TO WORK AT

Not every group or church has the resources, the time or the need for drama. It requires considerable investment of time by the right people, just like a choir. And like a choir, it's only worth doing well. These dramas take time to prepare and need some rehearsing.

69 THE JOB INTERVIEW

This can be used with 'Jesus and the First Disciples' on page 18. It works best with an audience which has some knowledge of who the disciples were, and which is able to pick up some of the biblical allusions.

CAST
Interviewer
Candidate 1
Candidate 2

POINT
The disciples, such as Simon Peter, our candidate number one, were the unlikely lads. The most impressive of them may have been candidate number two, Judas Iscariot. Jesus chose ordinary people like you and me to follow him, not the most talented or perfect. They were simply people ready to be taught and to follow where he led. And they weren't all perfect.

PREPARATION LEVEL
★★ or ★★★

Interviewer *(Calls out.)* Next please! *(Candidate enters.)* Are you here for the discipleship job?
Candidate 1 Certainly am.
Interviewer You know what it involves?
Candidate 1 Certainly do. You won't get a better disciple than me. I'm up for this one all right.
Interviewer Excuse me being personal, but what's that smell?
Candidate 1 Oh, that's probably the fish. Don't notice it myself. Just come from cleaning the nets.
Interviewer Right. Well, what makes you think you'd be a good disciple?
Candidate 1 No doubt about it, I'm the man Jesus needs in his team. Lay down my life for him, I would. I mean, I've already lent him my boat when he needed it. Being a fisherman, I'm good on water, wouldn't mind having another go at walking on it; and I know about fishes, so I could probably do the loaves and fishes business.
Interviewer Are you referring to the feeding of the five thousand?
Candidate 1 I didn't realize it was that many. Yeah, probably, but I'm a good leader, ready to dive in, take risks, I've got a loud voice and I wouldn't be afraid to tell people to repent, or else –
Interviewer Or else...?
Candidate 1 I'd, I'd, I'd... cut off their ear with a sword.
Interviewer I thought Jesus wants you to love your neighbour as yourself?
Candidate 1 Yeah, well, I have to talk to him about that. I think he's being a bit unrealistic there.
Interviewer Well, thank you very much for your time, sir. We shall be in touch. *(Candidate exits.)* Next!

Candidate 2 enters. He is very smart, efficient, wearing a suit and carrying a briefcase.

Candidate 2 I've come for the job interview. Disciple. Here's my CV.
Interviewer *(Reads it.)* Very impressive, I must say.
Candidate 2 I think I have all the right qualifications. Having been involved in the world of politics for some years now, I am committed to change and a better future for society. My personal manifesto is very close to that of Jesus, I too have come for the poor.

	I hate extravagance, and believe that money spent on modern luxuries, like perfume, should rather be donated to worthy causes.
Interviewer	So you think you can get on with Jesus over the long term, do you?
Candidate 2	I would be entirely committed to his aims of justice and equality. I think I would be an asset to his team. As my references show, I have vast experience in personnel management and budget control, and I have many contacts in high places.
Interviewer	Thank you very much for coming. I'm sure your application will receive the utmost attention from the rest of our panel here this morning.

(Candidate 2 exits. Interviewer turns to audience.)

Now, who's it to be? Will it be fishy number one? He has some strong ideas of his own, and he'd walk on water for you, even dive in fully-clothed. Sounds like he might have to if he's going to cool that hot temper of his. Or will it be organiser number two? He'll run your budget and personnel problems, and give you some great contacts of his own. Who would you choose to be your disciple?

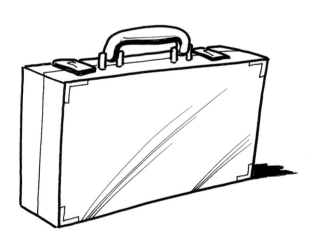

70 ALAS SMITH AND JONES

Could be a good laugh. Can be used as part of a cabaret evening on the subject of materialism, or linked with the Parable of the Rich Fool on page 21.

CAST
Smith
Jones

POINT
Everyone's talking about money these days. It can occupy our every waking thought and it's the subject of almost every conversation in pubs everywhere. This was the problem with the rich fool: it was all he could think about.

PREPARATION LEVEL
★★ or ★★★ Needs rehearsing and learning of lines

Smith and Jones are sitting on bar stools, drinking.

Smith You know what makes me sick?
Jones Badly-cooked hamburgers?
Smith The National Lottery.
Jones Why's that then?
Smith All those millions of people thinking they'll be happy if only they win.
Jones Well, they would be, wouldn't they?
Smith They'd be miserable. I mean, if you were a millionaire, the man who had everything, what would you want for Christmas?
Jones Erm, a burglar alarm, probably.
Smith You see, you'd be scared stiff you'd lose it all. Miserable you'd be.

(Pause.)

Jones It couldn't be you then? You don't buy any tickets?
Smith No. *(Pause.)* Well, not often. Just one a week. In case.
Jones In case what?
Smith In case I'm wrong, and you're not miserable.
Jones I won a couple of months back, you know.
Smith No!
Jones Just got a couple of grand.
Smith You were lucky.
Jones I was lucky and I was smart. You see, I like the number seven. And as it was the seventh month, July, I worked out seven times seven would come up. Smart, eh? So I put the number 48 down, and it came up.

(Pause.)

Smith But seven times seven is forty-nine.
Jones Yeah, that was the lucky bit.

(Pause.)

Smith But you know what really makes me sick? It's how people are only interested in you if you've got something they want. Become a millionaire, and suddenly you'd have hundreds of 'friends'. I mean, when was the last time you got a letter from someone interested in you?
Jones Got one this morning. A red-letter day it was. From East Midlands Electricity. Red all over it was.
Smith There you are! They only write when they want your money. No money, nobody'd ever talk to you again.
Jones *(Finishes his drink.)* Here, lend us a fiver. I'll get the next round in.

71 TALENTED

A dramatic way of presenting the parable of the talents. Good for bringing the reading alive in services where different ages are present. Narrators can read their lines.

CAST
Narrator 1
Narrator 2
Rich man
Servant 1
Servant 2
Servant 3

POINT
God has given you at least one talent. One day he will ask you how you used it. What sort of answer will you be able to give?

PREPARATION LEVEL
★★★ Needs rehearsing to make this effective

Narrator 1	Once upon a time there was a rich man *(actor turns round)* who had many servants.

(Three servants turn round and fall on one knee.)

Servants	Sir!
Narrator 2	The rich man was going on a long journey.
Narrator 1	So he called his servants to him.
Narrator 2	And distributed his wealth amongst them.
Narrator 1	To the first he gave five talents of money.
Rich man	Put this money to work. When I return, I will see what use you have made of it.
Servant 1	Sir! *(Bows down low.)*
Narrator 1	So with the money the servant bought a shop. Night and day he worked.
Narrator 2	Buying and selling.
Narrator 1	Lifting and carrying.
Narrator 2	Opening and closing.
Narrator 1	Haggling and bargaining.
Narrator 2	From dawn until dusk.

(Servant does the actions, ends asleep.)

Narrator 1	To his second servant the rich man gave two talents of money.
Rich man	Put this money to work. When I return, I will see what use you have made of it.
Servant 2	Sir! *(Bows down low.)*
Narrator 1	So the servant bought a field with the money. Night and day he worked.
Narrator 2	Weeding and hoeing.
Narrator 1	Ploughing and planting.
Narrator 2	Sowing and watering.
Narrator 1	Reaping and harvesting.
Narrator 2	From dawn until dusk.

(Servant does the actions, ends asleep.)

Narrator 1	To his third servant the rich man gave one talent of money.
Rich man	Put this money to work. When I return, I will see what use you have made of it.
Servant 3	Sir! *(Bows down low.)*
Narrator 1	Now the third servant didn't like shops.
Narrator 2	He didn't like fields.
Narrator 1	He didn't know what to do.
Narrator 2	So he dug a hole in the ground.
Narrator 1	And put his talent there, to keep it safe.
Narrator 2	And then he fell asleep.
Narrator 1	From dawn until dusk.
Narrator 2	Until one day, the master returned.

(All servants wake up.)

Narrator 1	He called his servants to him to see what had become of his wealth.

Servant 1	Sir, you entrusted me with five talents. See, I have gained five more.
Rich man	Well done, good and faithful servant! You have been faithful with a few things, I will put you in charge of many things. Come and share your master's happiness! *(Shakes his hand, congratulates him.)*
Servant 2	Sir, you entrusted me with two talents. See, I have gained two more.
Rich man	Well done, good and faithful servant! You have been faithful with a few things, I will put you in charge of many things. Come and share your master's happiness! *(Shakes his hand, congratulates him.)*
Servant 3	Sir, I was afraid and did not know what to do. So I went out and hid your talent in the ground. Here is what belongs to you.
Narrator 1	But his master was not impressed.
Narrator 2	He had him thrown out.
Rich man	Take the talent from him and give it to the one who has the ten talents. For everyone who has will be given more, and he will have an abundance. Whoever does not have, even what he has will be taken from him.

72 NICE ROLLS

Can be used to set the theme for the feeding of the five thousand. Can be followed directly by the Bible reading of the event without explanation. You need two good actors who can learn their lines and deliver them with good timing for this to work.

CAST
Ted
Harry
(Names and sex can be changed!)

POINT
God's miracles are not usually announced with a roll of drums and a fanfare. You can even be eating one and not notice!

PREPARATION LEVEL
★★★ Needs some rehearsal and talent

Ted and Harry are sitting down eating rolls.

Ted	Nice rolls these, Harry.
Harry	Mmmmm.

(Pause as they carry on eating.)

Ted	What's in 'em, Harry?
Harry	Dunno, Ted. Fish of some sort.

(Pause.)

Ted	What's the time, Harry?
Harry	*(Looks at watch. He is shocked.)* I don't believe it!
Ted	What's the matter?
Harry	It's nearly eight-thirty, Ted. What'll I tell the Missus now I'm late for supper?
Ted	Eight-thirty? You mean, we've been here... wait a minute... over four hours? No wonder I was feeling so peckish before we got these rolls.
Harry	I thought it was nearer six o'clock, Ted.
Ted	So did I, Harry, so did I. *(Pause.)* Good talker, though, ain't he?
Harry	Oh yes.
Ted	I mean, there's not many people I could listen to for four hours.
Harry	I like his stories. That one about the farmer, f'rinstance, sowing his seed. Never thought of meself as a bit of soil before, have you, Ted?

Ted	Can't say I have, Harry. *(Pause.)* You don't want to believe all you hear about him though.
Harry	How d'ya mean?
Ted	You know, all that rubbish about him touching people and they're cured, and him turning gallons of water into wine, and that sort of thing.
Harry	Yeah, I did hear something about that.
Ted	There's even talk he brought someone back to life. Dead as a doornail they were, and then he talks to them, and they're right as rain again. Ridiculous. Load of rubbish.
Harry	Yeah, ridiculous. Load of rubbish. *(Pause.)* Just one thing, though, Ted.
Ted	What's that, Harry?
Harry	I wonder where he got all these fish rolls from?

(Freeze for three seconds.) eating!

73 ALL STRESSED OUT

(Chorus is person from side of stage speaking into microphone. He/she speaks in the rhythm of a train)

POINT
The motto for today could well be, 'I am very busy, therefore I am.' We must beware of it; life does not consist in the abundance of busyness.

PREPARATION LEVEL
★★ Needs some rehearsal to make it effective.

Chorus	So little time, so much to do! So little time, so much to do! Get up, get up! Get up, get up! *(Actors asleep in middle of stage. They wake with a start. Mime putting on clothes, brushing teeth and hair, etc. Have a quick bite for breakfast.)*
Chorus	No time for breakfast, no time for breakfast! *(Actors now running on the spot, put on a coat, mime rushing out of the door and into car, often looking at watch, etc.)*
Chorus	Put your foot down, put your foot down! *(Actors suffer fits of road rage.)*
Chorus	It looks like you're late, it looks like you're late! *(Actors tear their hair out.)*
Chorus	Get to work, get to work! *(Actors mime writing things down, scratching heads, etc.)*
Chorus	So little time, so much to do! So little time, so much to do! *(Actors look at watch, write all the more furiously, read books.)*
Chorus	Time to go home, time to go home. Hurry, hurry! So little time, so much to do!
Actor	*(Starts speaking from seat in audience then goes up on stage.)* Excuse me, can you stop a minute? *(The two look at him as though he's crazy.)* I just wanted to ask you something. Have you got a moment? *(They shake their heads, look at each other and point to this guy as though he's from another planet.)* Look, I've been watching you all day. You run around like headless chickens. What are you doing it for? *(Actors can't understand him.)*
Chorus	*(Softly, then getting louder.)* So little time, so much to do; so little time, so much to do. *(Continues as actors rush off.)*
Actor	But what is there to do?

DRAMA FOR ALL SEASONS

74 CHRISTMAS: WORLD EXCLUSIVE

CAST
Reporter
Farmer George
Farmer Eric

POINT
However many nativity plays and carol services you go to, don't let familiarity take away the wonder that God chose this way of coming into the world. You could hardly find a more humble entrance than this, and one more open to misunderstanding.

PREPARATION LEVEL
★★★ This sketch needs little movement, so the characters need to be larger than life to hold interest and create humour.

Reporter enters with pen and notebook in hand, looking cold and dejected. She is speaking into portable phone.

Reporter Yes, sir. I'll do my best, sir... If there's a story here, I'll be the first to get it, and you'll be the first to know. *(She puts phone away.)* I do not believe it! Just because it's the national census, and I'm his star reporter, he expects me to find a front-page story. In this God-forsaken hole! *(Looks up to sky for inspiration.)* Oh, there's a bright star! I wonder what that's doing here? *(Farmer passes by.)* Excuse me, sir, are you local?

George Sort of. I live in the hills up there, sheep farmer. George is the name.

Reporter I don't suppose you know if there's any news going on here.

George News?

Reporter As in newspaper. I'm from the *Daily Spot*. Looking for sleaze, I mean news.

George Well, there is the national census. That's why the place is packed.

Reporter Yes, I know it's the census. But is anything unusual happening?

George Just seen a new-born baby. That any good?

Reporter Not exactly going to make the front page is it? 'World exclusive – baby born!'

George Only trying to help. I reckon he's pretty special myself. *(Farmer Eric passes by.)* Hi, Eric! Worth coming down for, wasn't it?

Eric Wouldn't have missed it for the world, George!

Reporter Excuse me, are you local?

Eric I'm from up in the hills. Like George here. Sheep farmer.

Reporter Look, I'm from the *Daily Spot*. I was wondering if there's anything unusual in town this evening?

Eric Well, as a matter of fact there is, isn't there George?

Reporter *(Gets notepad ready.)* Yes?

Eric It's the national census.

Reporter *(Sighing.)* Yes, I know it's the census. Well, thank you so much for your help.

George Of course, we have just seen a few kings, haven't we Eric?

Reporter Yes, and I'm the Queen of Sheba. I haven't got time for jokes.

Eric Visiting this baby boy they were. Just like the crowd of us shepherds. It seems like he's sort of special.

Reporter 'World exclusive – special baby born'. No, still doesn't work for a banner headline. *(Starts to leave.)*

Eric *(Calls after her.)* He was born in a cow-shed.

Reporter *(Stops.)* It's a start. 'Homeless baby born'. Hmmm, human interest there at least.

George The really strange thing is that none of us are sure who the father is – don't you think, Eric?

Reporter *(Starts to get excited.)* Did you say, you're not sure who the father is?

Eric That's right. I mean, the mother's not married yet and…

Reporter *(Interrupting.)* 'Census sensation – agony of betrayed young Mum!'

Eric Well, she seemed pretty happy actually. So did Joseph.

Reporter Joseph? Who's he?

George As far as we know, he's standing in for the real Dad. Sort of, erm, surrogate father. Carpenter he is.

Reporter ' "I forgive her", says chippy boyfriend'.

Eric And the kings were really nice, weren't they George?

Reporter 'Royals caught in stable scandal.' So there really were some kings?

George Yeah, and they all bowed down and gave him these amazing presents.

Reporter 'Crazy kings ripped off by love-child.'

Eric But even more amazing were all those angels.

Reporter 'Crazy kings and green welly brigade hallucinate in stable scandal.' Bit long, but I think it's promising.

Eric I know it sounds unlikely. It probably sounds pretty foolish to a sober reporter like yourself. The best thing is for you to go down to the cow-shed. Then you can see the baby and get the facts for yourself.

Reporter Oh, we needn't let the facts get in the way of a great story like this. Now, if you could just give me your names. *(She writes in notebook and they all freeze in position.)*

75 PENTECOST: THE PRESENT

CAST
Narrator
Actor

POINT
Apart from the first speech, the narrator's words are taken from Scripture. They make the point that we cannot understand God or participate in the life that he longs for us to have unless without the aid of his Spirit.

PREPARATION LEVEL
★★ The narrator remains quite deadpan throughout. The actor needs good timing and to say the words naturally rather than as a script learned parrot-fashion.

Narrator	Here is the present. It's for you. Beautiful, comforting, life-changing. Take it. *(Holds it out.)*
Actor	*(Comes on reading newspaper. Stands next to present not noticing it.)*
Narrator	But you didn't notice the present. And you never opened it. *(Puts it on table. Goes to stand at lectern.)*
Narrator	Jesus said, I will ask the Father, and he will give you another comforter, and he will never leave you. He is the Holy Spirit.
Actor	Seeing is believing. And I don't see anything.
Narrator	The world cannot accept him because it neither sees him nor knows him.
Actor	*(Turns his/her back on the present.)*
Narrator	When he, the Spirit of truth, comes, he will guide you into all truth.
Actor	*(Starts to walk down aisle.)* I know where I'm going. I've got my future all mapped out.
Narrator	When he comes he will convict the world of guilt in regard to sin and righteousness and judgement.
Actor	*(Has put hands over ears.)* I lead a good life, a Christian life, with Christian values.
Narrator	But when he, the Holy Spirit, has come upon you, you will receive power to testify about me with great effect.
Actor	No thank you, I certainly don't want to be one of those fanatical weirdoes preaching at everyone on street corners.
Narrator	The Spirit testifies with our spirit that we are God's children.
Actor	I'm just not sure who God is.
Narrator	By the Spirit we say 'Abba, Father'.
Actor	If you're not sure about God, it's hard to pray to him.
Narrator	The Spirit himself intercedes for us.
Actor	It's just all so confusing.
Narrator	Jesus said, 'Peace I leave you, my peace I give you.'

76 EASTER: AN EASY WAY OUT?

CAST
Reader
Person

POINT
The reader's words are from Scripture. Jesus has gone through the agony of Gethsemane and Calvary, so 'we have one who has been tempted in every way, just as we are'. We can turn to him 'so that we may receive mercy and find grace to help in time of need' (Hebrews 4:15,16).

PREPARATION LEVEL
★★ Take care not to play for laughs.

Actor stands centre. The reader stands to one side and speaks when the actor is in a frozen position.

Person I wish I knew what to do. I know I ought to really… It's just so hard. I don't know whether I can face up to it. I'm just not strong enough to go through with it. *(Freeze.)*

Reader Jesus took Peter and the two sons of Zebedee along with him, and he began to be sorrowful and troubled. Then he said to them, 'My soul is overwhelmed with sorrow to the point of death. Stay here and keep watch with me.'

Person I mean, it would be easier if someone were here to help me. Give some moral support, you know, that sort of thing. *(Freeze.)*

Reader Going a little further, Jesus fell with his face to the ground and prayed, 'My Father, if it is possible, may this cup be taken from me.'

Person *(Looking up.)* I can't believe you want me to do this. In fact, I've probably got it wrong. It's just my imagination. After all, we don't have to go seeking out suffering, just because we're Christians. We're justified by faith, not works. Aren't we? So me doing this isn't going to justify me, or get me brownie points with you. Is it? *(Freeze.)*

Reader Then he prayed, 'Yet not as I will, but as you will.'

Person And another thing – it says somewhere, 'You'll never be tempted more than you can bear.' I remember that. It's there somewhere. We did it in a Bible study once. So this can't be what you want. I can't take it. OK? *(Exits.)*

Reader Then Jesus returned to his disciples and found them sleeping. 'Could you men not keep watch with me for one hour?' he asked Peter. 'Watch and pray so that you will not fall into temptation. The spirit is willing, but the body is weak.'

INDEX

Items in **bold** refer to major biblical passages or theological themes. The rest are subjects alluded to, or objects used, in the illustrations.

The numbers refer to the illustrations, not to the pages.

Advertisements	49, 50
Appearances	34-36
Borrowed book	45
Busyness	73
Chinese whispers	29
Christmas	74
Comparisons	32
Compassion	11
Confession	27
Control	52
Crucifixion	59
Death	13-20
Desperation	1
Disciples of Jesus	38-42, 62, 69
Discipleship	39, 41, 62, 67
DIY	47
Doll	10
Drink	4, 5, 6
Easter	59, 76
Effort	16
Failure	1, 2, 46
Fear	46
Feeding the 5,000	8-11, 72
Food	8
Forgiveness	54-57, 63, 64
Fishing	40
Gethsemane	76
Gifts	43, 44, 64, 65
Guess who?	26
Happy endings	15
Hard questions	17, 24
Heart, cold	31
Helping each other	42
Impossibilities	38
Jigsaws	21
Knots	20, 24
Listening to God	59
Loose ends	25
Marbles	17
Miracles	1-6, 8-11, 13-20, 72
Mirrors	30
Missing piece	23
Music	38
Mystery	44
New life	15, 19, 20
Nicodemus	21-27, 68
Pentecost	65, 75
Perseverance	18
Possessions	49-53, 70
Raising of Lazarus	13-20
Resurrection	13-20, 59
Rich fool	49-53, 68, 70
Sand bucket	57
Secrets	10
Self-image	36
Simon says	39, 67
Sport	32, 51, 66
Suffering	61, 76
Talents	43-48, 66, 71
Targets	53
Thumbprints	9
Tramps	34
Unforgiving servant	54-57, 63, 64
Uniqueness	9
Waiting	37
Water	4
Wedding at Cana	1-6
Weights	42
Wine	4
Zacchaeus	29-32, 60

CPAS Church Pastoral Aid Society is an Anglican mission agency helping churches make disciples of Jesus Christ.

We work across Great Britain and Ireland to resource local churches and their leaders for mission and evangelism. We affirm the supremacy of Scripture in all that we do.

1. Evangelism

Our evangelists help church members, both ordained and lay, to become more effective in their individual and corporate Christian witness. We aim to provide all the evangelism help a local church might need, including training and resources in personal evangelism for adults and children, church planting, conducting missions, reaching the unchurched and helping the church become a missionary congregation. All of this is carefully tailored to the practical needs and realities of the community in which the church lives. We also train evangelists for regional and national ministry.

2. Local Church Leadership for Mission

Our work is focused on enabling and supporting a missionary leadership in the local church. We seek to enable churches to become missionary congregations by providing a wide range of help to clergy, Readers, evangelists, churchwardens, church councils, and locally recognized leaders such as youth workers, leaders of youth and children's groups and of home groups. In addition to providing national, regional and local training events, we work increasingly with individuals and small groups of leaders. We help people discover what leadership role God is calling them to, and we support them with a range of mission-oriented training and resources once they are in post.

Patronage: We nominate incumbents to over 500 parishes and thereby seek to ensure a continuity of gospel ministry in those parishes (we are the largest Patron in the Church of England after the Crown).

Grants: We make substantial grants each year to help churches pay for additional people to work with existing church leaders, especially in inner city and rural areas.

3. Young People, Children and Families

Over 2,000 churches have over 100,000 young people and children in groups supported by CPAS with biblical teaching, resources and training. We call these groups *CYFA* (14s to 18s), *Pathfinders* (11s to 14s), *Explorers* (7s to 11s), *Climbers* (5s to 7s) and *Scramblers* (3s to 5s), although sometimes local churches use different names. We also help churches start and maintain groups for families and under fives. In addition to training events our team of specialists in Head Office and in the regions work on an individual and continuing basis with church and group leaders. We help them bring the gospel of Christ to all these varied groups. We arrange camps and houseparties, called *Ventures* and *Falcon Camps,* for over 10,000 leaders, young people and children each year. Our vision is to see 150,000 children and young people in groups we support by the end of the millennium.

4. Publications

We publish resource materials with a mission orientation on important practical themes of Christian ministry. All are subsidized to help churches and leaders afford them. They are increasingly used by Anglican and non-Anglican churches.

Encouraging Mission, Resourcing Leaders

Our vision is to develop as a quality mission agency helping churches to make disciples of Jesus Christ.